S0-ACQ-825

APR 2003

Tasting

CHELSEA CLUBHOUSE

An Imprint of Chelsea House Publishers

A Haights Cross Communications Company

Philadelphia

Kimberley Jane Pryor

For Nick, Ashley and Thomas

This edition first published in 2004 in the United States of America by Chelsea Clubhouse, a division of Chelsea House Publishers and a subsidiary of Haights Cross Communications.

All rights reserved. No part of this publication may be reproduced or transmitted in any form or by any means without the written permission of the publisher.

Chelsea Clubhouse
1974 Sproul Road, Suite 400
Broomall, PA 19008-0914

The Chelsea House world wide web address is www.chelseahouse.com

Library of Congress Cataloging-in-Publication Data

Pryor, Kimberley Jane.
    Tasting / Kimberley Jane Pryor.
    p. cm. — (The senses)

    Includes index.
    Contents: Your senses — Your tongue — Taste buds — A message to your brain — All kinds of tastes — Tasting danger — Smell and taste — Touch and taste — Sight and taste — Protecting your tongue — Using all your senses.

    ISBN 0-7910-7557-5
    1. Taste—Juvenile literature. [1. Taste. 2. Tongue. 3. Senses and sensation.] I. Title. II. Series.
    QP456.P79 2004
    612.8'7—dc21

                                                                                    2003001176

First published in 2003 by
MACMILLAN EDUCATION AUSTRALIA PTY LTD
627 Chapel Street, South Yarra, Australia, 3141

Associated companies and representatives throughout the world.

Copyright © Kimberley Jane Pryor 2003

Page layout by Raul Diche
Illustrations by Alan Laver, Shelly Communications
Photo research by Legend Images

Printed in China

Acknowledgements
Cover photograph: children eating watermelon, courtesy of Photodisc.

Artville, pp. 14 (bottom left), 20; Corbis Digital Stock, p. 14 (top right); Getty Images/Image Bank, p. 21; Getty Images/Stone, p. 24; Getty Images/Taxi, pp. 7, 10, 12; Great Southern Stock, pp. 5, 9, 16, 17, 25, 26, 27, 28, 29; Nick Milton, pp. 6, 23; Photodisc, pp. 1, 4, 13, 14 (top left and bottom right), 15; Photolibrary.com/SPL, p. 8; Terry Oakley/The Picture Source, p. 18.

While every care has been taken to trace and acknowledge copyright, the publisher tenders their apologies for any accidental infringement where copyright has proved untraceable. Where the attempt has been unsuccessful, the publisher welcomes information that would redress the situation.

Please note
At the time of printing, the Internet addresses appearing in this book were correct. Owing to the dynamic nature of the Internet, however, we cannot guarantee that all these addresses will remain correct.

J 612.8 P956t 2004
Pryor, Kimberley Jane.
Tasting

Contents

Your Senses

You have five senses to help you learn about the world. They are taste, sight, hearing, smell, and touch.

You taste watermelon with your tongue.

Tasting

You taste things with your tongue. Your sense of taste helps you to choose and enjoy food. It also warns you of danger.

Your tongue tells you if something tastes bad.

Your Tongue

Your tongue is made of muscle **tissue** and is covered by a **mucous membrane**. The mucous membrane makes a wet, slimy liquid called mucus.

Your tongue is attached to the bottom of your mouth by the **frenulum**. Your tongue is also attached to your throat.

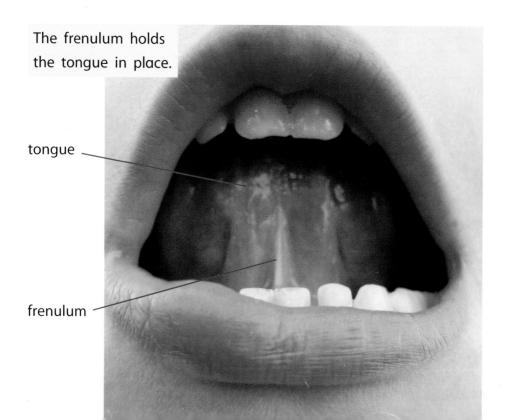

The frenulum holds the tongue in place.

tongue

frenulum

Your tongue helps make the shape of the words you sing.

Your tongue bends easily. It moves food from the front to the back of your mouth and helps you to swallow. It also helps you to talk and sing.

7

On the surface of your tongue, you can see tiny bumps called **papillae**. Papillae help you to grip your food. They also have receptor cells called **taste buds**, which sense the different tastes in foods.

papillae   taste buds

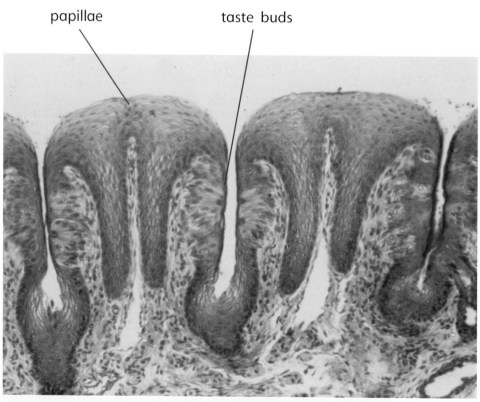

Most of the papillae on your tongue have taste buds.

There are four types of papillae, but only three kinds have taste buds. The papillae with taste buds each have a different location:

✪ far back on the tongue
✪ on the sides of the tongue toward the back
✪ on the front sides and tip of the tongue.

The papillae you see in the center of your tongue do not have taste buds.

The papillae that have taste buds are located in these areas on the tongue.

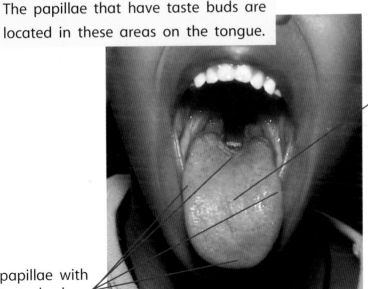

papillae without taste buds

papillae with taste buds

Taste Buds

You have about 10,000 taste buds on your tongue. A few taste buds are also found on the roof of the mouth and in the throat. A taste bud is a group of 50 to 100 taste cells that fit together like the segments of an orange.

Children have more taste buds than older people.

When you eat, food **dissolves** in your **saliva**. Bits of dissolved food enter a taste bud through a tiny **taste pore** and touch taste hairs on the taste cells. The cells sense the taste and send signals along a nerve to the brain.

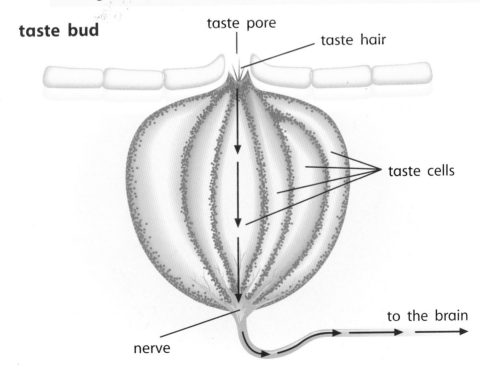

Messages from taste cells travel along a nerve to the brain.

taste bud

taste pore

taste hair

taste cells

to the brain

nerve

A Message to Your Brain

The taste and the smell of food work together. The brain uses messages from your tongue and your nose to decide what the food's **flavor** is, whether you like it, and if you should eat more.

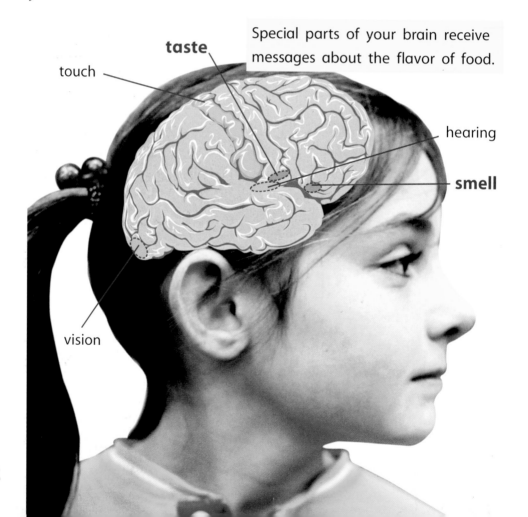

touch

taste

Special parts of your brain receive messages about the flavor of food.

hearing

smell

vision

When you taste a cookie, cells in your tongue and nose send messages to your brain. Then your brain sends a message to your mouth to eat more of the cookie.

Your nose and your tongue help you to know that a cookie tastes good.

All Kinds of Tastes

Most scientists agree that there are four main tastes:

- ✪ sweet
- ✪ sour
- ✪ salty
- ✪ bitter.

Some scientists believe there is a fifth taste, called **umami**. Umami is described as a meaty taste.

Sweet

Salty

Sour

Bitter

Sweet tastes

Most people like foods that taste sweet, such as strawberries, watermelon, and honey. Some people add sugar to foods and drinks because they like sweet tastes. Sweet foods are often high in energy.

Party foods, such as cake and ice cream, are often sweet.

Salty tastes

Many people like foods that taste salty, such as soup, pretzels, and crackers. Some people add salt to their food because they like salty tastes. However, too much salt can be harmful to people with some illnesses.

Potato chips and other snacks can be very salty.

Sour tastes

Some foods have a sour taste, such as lemons and vinegar. People may like some sour tastes. However, sour tastes also tell us when a food or drink may have gone bad.

Spoiled milk tastes sour.

Bitter and umami tastes

Foods and drinks that have a bitter taste include grapefruit, coffee, and tonic water. Foods that have the umami taste are meat, fish, and cheese.

Some people like the bitter taste of grapefruit.

Try this!

Ask a parent or teacher for help.

Taste match

- Collect several foods or drinks that are sweet, salty, sour, or bitter.

- Ask a friend to close his or her eyes and to taste each food or drink.

- Ask, "What taste does this food or drink have?"

- Can your friend tell if the foods or drinks are sweet, salty, sour, or bitter?

Taste chart			
Sweet	**Salty**	**Sour**	**Bitter**
strawberries	potato chips	lime	grapefruit
sugar	corn chips	vinegar	cold coffee
honey	pretzels	sour candies	tonic water
fruit juice	popcorn	lemon juice	onion juice

Tasting Danger

Your sense of taste sometimes warns you of danger. It may tell you if food is no longer safe to eat. If a food tastes different than normal, it may be spoiled or unsafe to eat.

Unripened bananas may taste bitter and could make your stomach upset.

You may want to taste new foods slowly.

If you have never tried a food before, you may want to taste it slowly. If it tastes bad, or if it makes you feel funny, you should stop eating it.

Smell and Taste

Your brain uses messages about the smell and the taste of food to decide its flavor. If you have a bad cold, foods may not seem to have as much flavor. This is because your nose cannot smell the food as well.

Your brain receives messages about the flavor of food from your nasal cavity and mouth.

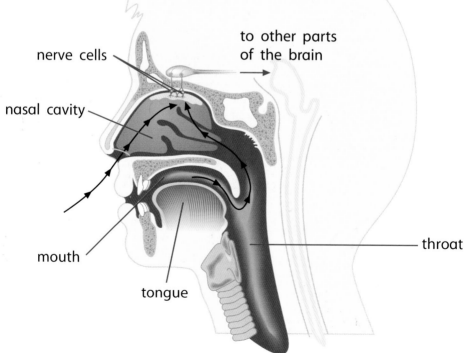

nerve cells

to other parts of the brain

nasal cavity

mouth

tongue

throat

Try this!

Ask a parent or teacher for help.

Apple or pear?

- ✪ Cut a piece of apple and a piece of pear and place them on a plate.

- ✪ Close your eyes and hold your nose shut.

- ✪ Lick one of the pieces of fruit. Can you tell which one it is?

- ✪ Now let go of your nose and lick the same piece. Can you tell which one it is now?

You will see how your sense of smell helps you tell what something tastes like.

Your sense of smell helps you tell which fruit you are tasting.

Touch and Taste

You use your sense of touch when you eat and drink. When you eat, your tongue feels the food. Your tongue tells you whether the food feels smooth or rough, hot or cold, wet or dry, and soft or hard.

Ice cream is smooth and cold.

Try this!

Ask a parent or teacher for help.

Fruit cubes

✪ Collect fruits that are similar in color, smoothness, temperature, wetness, and hardness, such as peach, nectarine, mango, and cantalope.

✪ Cut the fruit into small cubes.

✪ Ask a friend to taste each fruit.

✪ Ask, "What fruit is this?"

Can your friend tell what each fruit is by its taste?

Foods that feel the same on your tongue may be hard to tell apart.

Sight and Taste

The look of food may make you expect a certain taste. If a drink looks orange, you may expect it to have an orange taste. The look of food may also tell you if it is spoiled. Bread or cheese that is bad may have green, fuzzy spots.

Food that is burned may not be safe to eat.

Try this!

Ask a parent or teacher for help.

Color test

⭐ Fill two cups with water.

⭐ Add orange food coloring to one cup of water. The orange water will have color but no flavor.

⭐ Ask a friend to try each cup of water.

⭐ Ask, "What does the drink taste like?"

Your friend might say the orange water tastes like oranges because it looks like an orange-flavored drink.

The color of a drink may seem to change its flavor.

Protecting Your Tongue

Your sense of taste is important and helps you to enjoy food and drink. So, protect your tongue to keep it healthy!

⭐ Let hot foods and drinks cool down before you taste them.

⭐ Never put sharp objects into your mouth.

Let food cool down before you taste it.

Brush your tongue with a soft toothbrush.

You can keep your tongue clean by brushing
it gently when you brush your teeth.

Using All Your Senses

You need your senses to taste, see, hear, smell, and touch things. The best way to learn about the world is to use all your senses.

Did You Know?
Temperature changes how something tastes. If you suck on an ice cube before you take medicine, you will not taste the medicine as much.

Did You Know?
Older people have fewer taste buds than younger people. They may prefer salty or spicy foods, because these foods have more "taste".

Did You Know?
Catfish have taste buds all over their bodies to help them find food in muddy water.

Glossary

dissolves	mixes something in a liquid so that it becomes part of the liquid
flavor	the message the brain receives from both the smell and taste of a food or drink
frenulum	tissue that connects the tongue to the bottom of the mouth; the frenulum keeps the tongue from falling back into the throat.
mucous membrane	a thin tissue that covers the tongue and produces a liquid called mucus
papillae	the small bumps on the top and sides of the tongue that grip food; three of the four kinds of papillae have taste buds.
saliva	a liquid in the mouth that mixes with food
taste buds	tiny, bulb-shaped groups of cells that sense taste; taste buds can only be seen under a microscope.
taste pore	the tiny opening through which little bits of dissolved food enter a taste bud
tissue	a group of cells that forms a part of a plant, or an animal's or a person's body, such as a heart or muscle; the tongue is made of muscle tissue.
umami	a fifth taste that can be sensed by taste cells; umami is described as a meaty or savory taste; the food additive MSG triggers the umami taste.

Index

Web Sites

You can go to these web sites to learn more about the sense of taste:

http://www.kidshealth.org/kid/body/tongue_SW.html

http://faculty.washington.edu/chudler/tasty.html